Heroes and Villains of the

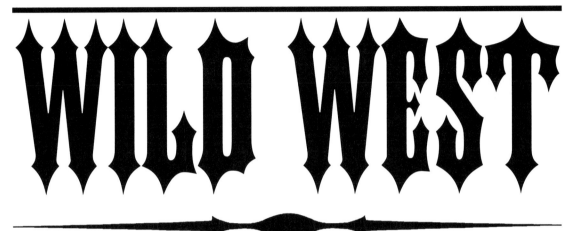

WILD WEST

Buffalo Bill Cody

by John Hamilton

ABDO & Daughters
PUBLISHING

Published by Abdo & Daughters, 4940 Viking Dr., Suite 622, Edina, MN 55435.

Copyright ©1996 by Abdo Consulting Group, Inc., Pentagon Tower, P.O. Box 36036, Minneapolis, Minnesota 55435. International copyrights reserved in all countries. No part of this book may be reproduced in any form without written permission from the publisher. Printed in the United States.

Cover Photo by: Bettmann
Inside Photos by:
Bettmann: pp. 23, 24, 25
Archive Photos: pp. 5, 9, 11, 15, 17, 19, 20
AP/Wide World Photos: pp. 13, 26, 27, 28
John Hamilton: p. 22

Edited by Ken Berg

Library of Congress Cataloging–in–Publication Data
Hamilton, John, 1959-
   "Buffalo Bill" Cody / written by John Hamilton
   p. cm. — (Heroes & villains of the wild west)
Includes bibliographical references and index.
ISBN: 1-56239-561-0
1. Buffalo Bill, 1846-1917—Juvenile literature. 2. Pioneers—West (U.S.)—Biography—Juvenile literature. 3. Entertainers—United States—Biography—Juvenile literature. 4. Buffalo Bill's Wild West Show—History—Juvenile literature. I. Title. II. Series.
F594.B94H36 1996
978'02'092—dc20   95-25038
[b]   CIP
                                                         AC

Contents

Introduction

 Autumn, 1864. The Civil War rages. A brawny 18-year-old scout for the 7th Kansas Volunteer Cavalry rides alone in western Missouri, enemy territory. The scout's name is William Cody, later to be known as "Buffalo Bill." This day he wears "Missouri jeans," plain gray clothes allowing him to evade detection as a Union soldier. His mission is to ride far ahead of the rest of his brigade and search out Rebel troops raiding the countryside.

Young Will rides up to a small farmhouse and stops. Upon entering through an open door, he suddenly freezes, his muscles tightening. Sitting at a table eating bread and milk is a Confederate officer. The man looks up, smiles and says, "You little rascal, what are you doing in those 'secesh' clothes?"

Will, without hesitation, replies, "I ask you the same question, sir." The "officer" is none other than Wild Bill Hickok, an old friend from Will's youth in Kansas.

Wild Bill waves off the younger man. "Hush! Sit down and have some bread and milk, and we'll talk afterwards." After eating and paying the woman of the house, the two walk out to the gate where Will's horse is tied. Will learns that Hickok, too, is an Army scout, dressing as a Confederate officer to spy on nearby troops. He gives Will a packet of information about Confederate movements and tells young Cody to deliver it to General McNiel.

"All right," Cody says, mounting his horse. "But where will I meet you again?"

"Never mind that," Hickok replies. "I'm getting so much valuable information that I propose to stay a little while longer in this disguise."

The pair shake hands and part, Will riding hard for his military station with the precious cargo in his saddlebag.

William "Buffalo Bill" Cody.

A true story? Nobody can say for sure. The record shows that Buffalo Bill did serve in the 7th Kansas Cavalry during the time described, and that Hickok was a Union spy. The only authority of the above story, however, lies in William Cody's own autobiography, "The Life of Buffalo Bill," a ripping yarn filled with the daring deeds of his earlier days.

What is certain is that Buffalo Bill's life was thrilling beyond measure. He had more adventures by the time he was a teenager than most of us will ever know. (At 14, after all, Cody was already an accomplished Pony Express rider.) A genuine frontier buffalo hunter, U.S. Army scout and Indian tracker, Cody symbolized the American West through real-life feats and later through fiction and drama with his famous Wild West show.

Early Kansas Days

William Frederick Cody was born in Scott County, Iowa, on February 26, 1846. "My debut upon the world's stage," as Will put it. Eight years later, Isaac Cody moved his family—wife, five daughters, and son Will—to Kansas, which was then a wild territory full of danger and opportunity. Will's father opened a trading post near Fort Leavenworth, doing business with friendly Kickapoo Indians. He also was active in politics, often traveling east to encourage abolitionists (those against slavery) to settle in Kansas. Pro-slavery thugs targeted the Codys because of Isaac's views. Isaac once was stabbed with a Bowie knife while giving an anti-slavery speech. He never fully recovered from the wound. The violence in Kansas was a preview of much bigger things to come years later, during the American Civil War.

It was in Kansas that young Will received his first horse and gun at age eight. His cousin, circus rider Horace Billings, helped break the horse, called Prince, and taught Will how to shoot from the saddle while at a full gallop. Billings was a hero in young Will's eyes. Will wanted to follow in his footsteps.

Will's early days in Kansas also held another great influence: His father's dealings with the Indians exposed the boy to the rich heritage of the Plains people. He spent time with Indian boys who taught him to use the bow and arrow, and how to play their games and sports. He even learned to talk the Kickapoo language to some extent.

Will's father held a Fourth of July barbecue for his Indian customers and his white neighbors and relatives. Said Will, "There were about two hundred Indians in attendance at the feast, and they all enjoyed and appreciated it. In the evening they had one of their grand, fantastic war dances, which greatly amused me, it being the first sight of the kind I had ever witnessed."

Earning a Living in the Saddle

By the time Will's father died in 1857, 11-year-old Cody was already a capable horseback rider and a good marksman. His first job had been with the freight company of Russel, Majors, and Waddell riding messages between Leavenworth and the fort three miles away. When his father died, young Will took the role of "man of the family." Over his mother's objections, he joined a cattle drive headed for Salt Lake City, Utah.

During the trip hostile Indians attacked the party, killing three men and scattering the herd. Cody and the rest of the men made it to a river a short distance away and started wading downstream, using the steep bank as protection. "I being the youngest," Will wrote, "and smallest of the party, became somewhat tired, and without noticing it I had fallen behind the others for some little distance. It was about ten o'clock and we were keeping very quiet and hugging close to the bank, when I happened to look up to the moonlit sky and saw the plumed head of an Indian peeping over the bank...I instantly aimed my gun at the head and fired. The report rang out sharp and loud on the night air, and was immediately followed by an Indian whoop, and the next moment about six feet of dead Indian came tumbling into the river. I was not only overcome with astonishment, but was badly scared, as I could hardly realize what I had done." Later, the *Leavenworth Times* newspaper reported the incident, putting young Cody in the spotlight for the first time.

It was on another such wagon train that Will first met his friend Wild Bill Hickok. Though 10 years older, the famed frontiersman took young Cody under his wing. Their friendship lasted for many years, until Wild Bill's death in Deadwood, Dakota Territory (now South Dakota) in 1876.

After this taste of adventure, nothing his mother could say would keep young Buffalo Bill at home. His life belonged on the Plains.

Buffalo Bill to the rescue.

Pony Express Rider

After several years with the freight company, including numerous run-ins with bandits and unfriendly Indians, Will was ready to move on. In 1860, at age 14, he began a stint with the famous Pony Express. The "Boy Wonder" of the Pony Express, they called him. The swift riding that was required (at least 15 miles an hour) was enough to make any normal man's teeth shake loose. But Will seemed to have a knack for the challenge, and more endurance than most of the older riders. After a couple months of outstanding work, he was assigned a 76-mile run through dangerous Indian territory.

One day, he came galloping into his home station and found that his relief rider had gotten into a drunken brawl the night before and wound up dead. Not hesitating, Will proceeded on to the next station, 86 miles away. He then turned around immediately and made the round trip without incident—322 miles on horseback at full speed in just over 21 hours. No rider ever broke this record during the existence of the Pony Express.

The Scout of the Plains

In 1863, Will's mother died of tuberculosis. Leaving the family home in the care of his sister Julia and her husband, Will joined the U.S. Army. He was soon assigned as a soldier-scout because of his courage, endurance, and remarkable tracking ability. (Patriotic fervor didn't exactly grip Cody, however. "I had no idea of doing anything of the kind," he said, "but one day, after having been under the influence of bad whiskey, I awoke to find myself a soldier in the 7th Kansas. I did not remember how or when I had enlisted, but I saw I was in for it, and that it would not do for me to endeavor to back out.")

After 18 months, Will was discharged. Shortly after, intent to settle down, he married Louisa Frederici (Lulu). For a few months he operated a hotel, but this "proved too tame." (He also proved to be a poor businessman, with little head for money matters.) Longing for a life on the

General Custer.

open Plains again, he settled his wife in Leavenworth with his sister Helen, and rode west for Saline, Kansas, at that time the end of the track of the Kansas Pacific Railway. For the rest of his life, Will rarely spent more than a few months home with his wife and the four children that arrived over the years. Lulu resented her part-time husband and the time he spent on the road, and their marriage would prove to alternate between periods of squabbling and affection.

During the next few years Cody worked as a civilian scout. The frontier was opening up, railroads were creeping west, and jobs were there for the taking. He guided many famous military heroes across the prairies, including Generals William T. Sherman and George A. Custer.

Buffalo Bill

Will Cody soon gained fame not only as a scout and Indian tracker, but as a buffalo hunter as well. His horse at the time was named Brigham, and was trained for hunting. One day a small herd was spotted not far from a work camp where Will was currently employed. Anxious for fresh meat, Will grabbed his .50-caliber Springfield rifle (which he named Lucretia Borgia) and started out to get dinner. Before he reached the herd, a small group of officers from nearby Fort Hays, Kansas, rode up to Cody.

"Hello, friend," said the captain. "I see you're out after the same game we are." Will replied that yes, he was hunting buffalo, too. The officers studied Will and his shabby outfit and laughed. "How do you expect to catch buffalo on that sad-looking horse?" they taunted. "You'll never catch them in the world, my fine fellow." In a condescending manner, they told Cody he could tag along and keep the scraps if he wished.

Cody gave the officers a head start. Then, seeing that the herd of buffalo would soon turn toward a creek, he sped forward to cut them off and overtake the soldiers.

In his autobiography, Cody wrote, "The buffaloes came rushing past me not a hundred yards distant, with the officers about three hundred yards in the rear. Now, thought I, is the time to 'get my work in,' as they say; and I pulled the blind-bridle from my horse, who knew as well as I did that we were out for buffaloes—as he was a trained hunter. The moment the bridle was off, he started at the top of his speed, running in ahead of the officers, and with a few jumps he brought me alongside of the rear buffalo. Raising old "Lucretia Borgia" to my shoulder, I fired, and killed the animal at the first shot. My horse then carried me alongside the next one, not ten feet away, and I dropped him at the next fire.

"As soon as one buffalo would fall, Brigham would take me so close to the next, that I could almost touch it with my gun. In this manner I killed the eleven buffaloes with twelve shots; and, as the last animal dropped, my horse stopped."

A herd of buffalo. Males, like the one in front, can weigh 2,400 pounds.

Dismounting, Cody presented himself to the astonished officers. After presenting them with the tongues and tenderloins (the tastiest bits), the troopers hailed Cody as "Buffalo Bill."

Or so the story goes.

Another version of how Buffalo Bill got his name comes from a job he later took with the railroad, which was at that time laying track to Sheridan, Kansas. Hired for a tidy sum of $500 a month, Cody's job was to provide 12 buffalo a day to the railroad's work crews. Of course, after a while this menu grew rather tiresome, eating buffalo day after day. When Will would come in off the Plains with his allotted number of carcasses, the workers would groan and lament, "Here comes that old Buffalo Bill."

During this stint with the railroad, Cody killed 4,280 buffalo in a period of 18 months, including a record 69 in one afternoon. His technique exploited the buffalo's instinct to follow the leader, rather than scatter in many different directions. Cody would ride up front, shooting the leaders and crowding the others until they started running in circles. Following close on the outside, Cody would then kill all he needed on that particular day.

By the early 1900's, out-of-control hunting had reduced the buffalo population to near extinction. Once they had numbered 70 million, with some herds stretching for miles. While Bill Cody hunted for meat to feed railway workers, others hunted the buffalo for the animals' prized skins. Millions were slaughtered, skinned, and left on the prairie to rot. Cody responded by becoming a conservationist, urging protection of the animals. He included buffalo in his Wild West show, and by 1890 his herd of 18 was the largest in captivity. Today, thankfully, buffalo have been restored to herd proportions, and are no longer endangered.

Chief of Scouts

In 1868, a bloody settler/Indian war erupted on the treeless Plains of Kansas. General Sheridan sent out a call for Buffalo Bill, appointing Cody as Chief of Scouts of the Fifth Cavalry. His tracking ability, courage, and dead eye with a gun made him the most valued scout on the frontier. He once led troops through a blinding snowstorm to rescue a lost group of soldiers trapped in the Texas Panhandle. (Among those isolated was Cody's old friend, Wild Bill Hickok. It was a happy reunion!) He rode many other expeditions through hostile Indian territory, sometimes in the dark of night. He survived countless battles with warriors of the Sioux and Cheyenne tribes.

During this time in history, white settlements were pushing far west of the Mississippi River, encroaching on Indian domain. Naturally, the proud Indian people resisted this invasion of their lands. Many white people, on the other hand, viewed the Indians as uncivilized and unchristian heathens who didn't deserve the status of nationhood. The whites felt the land was theirs for the taking. The battles that followed were inevitable.

Chief Sitting Bull

Buffalo Bill Cody knew Native Americans well, respecting both the people and their culture. While religious reformers argued that Indians should be kept on reservations, go to white-style schools, and adopt white ways, Cody wanted to help preserve Indian traditions. He also spoke out against government mistreatment on the reservations. Later in life, he employed many Indians to act in his Wild West show. (He considered Chief Sitting Bull, who was in the show for a year, his close friend.)

One time Cody got in trouble with the government for taking the Indians off their reservation. Cody argued that, rather than keep the two races separate, each would benefit through cultural exchange. He won his case, and the show went on. Chief Rocky Bear of the Sioux Nation once wrote to Cody, "I know you are a friend of the Indians."

It was this intimate knowledge of Indian habits and lore that made Cody so dangerous when it came to tracking them down. Though he respected them, he never hesitated to track down Indians that went on the warpath and terrorized settlers. Whether or not the Indians were justified in their attacks, they had a terrible foe in Buffalo Bill Cody when the game was afoot. The Sioux called him "Pahaska" (Long Hair), and he was much feared and respected as a warrior.

In 1869, Cody helped plan a surprise attack on Cheyenne Chief Tall Bull, which became the Battle of Summit Springs, Colorado. Tall Bull and his people had been raiding Kansas settlements, and Cody was hired to track him down. Guiding the troops into position around the Indian camp, Cody made the attack a total surprise. During the battle, Cody shot a warrior so as to confiscate his magnificent white horse. Only later did he learn he had killed the leader, Tall Bull, himself. Rescued was one of two white women who had earlier been kidnapped by the Cheyenne. The other woman was killed in the attack.

Cody in buckskins, brandishing the weapons of a Plains scout.

Hunting Parties

During the 1870's, Bill Cody bought land near North Platte, Nebraska, and built a complex he called "Scout's Rest," one of the finest ranches in the state. Here he settled down with his family. Or at least tried to. Not a man to sit in one place for very long, Cody was constantly out on the frontier, leading government troops through hostile territory, or guiding hunting parties of rich socialites from back East.

One such party in 1872 included Grand Duke Alexis of Russia, who had traveled to the Plains to get a taste of the famous American West. Cody went to great lengths to prepare for the hunting party, including coaxing about 100 friendly Sioux to put on a show of Indian culture and hunting skills. One morning the Duke was determined to hunt buffalo. Will gave the Duke his favorite horse at the time, Buckskin Joe, and they set out together.

Cody, in his autobiography, wrote, "Of course the main thing was to give Alexis the first chance and the best shot at the buffaloes, and when all was in readiness we dashed over a little knoll that had hidden us from view, and in a few minutes we were among them. Alexis at first preferred to use his pistol instead of a gun. He fired six shots from this weapon at buffaloes only twenty feet away from him, but as he shot wildly, not one of his bullets took effect. Riding up to his side and seeing that his weapon was empty, I exchanged pistols with him. He again fired six shots, without dropping a buffalo.

"Seeing that the animals were bound to make their escape without his killing one of them, unless he had a better weapon, I rode up to him, gave him my old reliable "Lucretia," and told him to urge his horse close to the buffaloes, and I would then give him the word when to shoot. At the same time I gave old Buckskin Joe a blow with my whip, and with a few jumps the horse carried the Grand Duke to within about ten feet of a big buffalo bull... He fired, and down went the buffalo."

Buffalo Bill out on an expedition.

Soon corks began to fly from champagne bottles as the party celebrated the Duke's first buffalo kill. Alexis was so impressed with Cody that he later gave the scout a diamond-encrusted buffalo-head pin and a robe of rare Siberian furs.

Because of his chosen profession, Cody didn't spend a lot of time with his family. Things grew more tense over the years between he and his wife. Though he considered divorce for quite some time, he remained married to Lulu until his death. Together they had four children: Orra, Arta, Irma, and Kit Carson (named after the famous scout). Orra and Kit died of childhood diseases, which was not uncommon in those days. He named a hotel for his youngest daughter Irma, in the town he helped build: Cody, Wyoming. (Bill thought the area, the eastern gateway to Yellowstone National Park, would be a splendid locale for tourism, ranching, and farming.)

Cody with his wife
Lulu in 1910.

The Wild West of
Buffalo Bill Cody

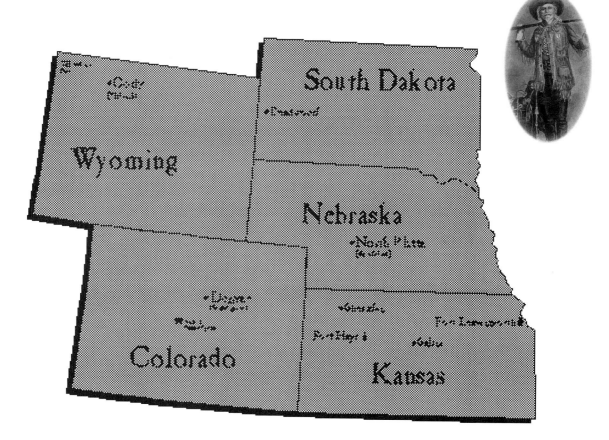

Show Business

Starting in the late 1870's, Buffalo Bill toured the East starring in rip-snorting Western dramas. One of the first was called "The Scouts of the Plains," and starred Cody together with his friend and fellow scout, Texas Jack Omohundro. The show opened with roaring success in Chicago, Illinois. Short on plot, and with terrible acting, the shows were little more than vehicles for Cody to act out thrilling stories of Western adventure. Though an awful actor, Cody was a superb showman, and knew what the public wanted to see. Audiences loved it, and the money poured in.

But the Plains held an undying allure for Cody. Still a young man, he longed for wide open spaces. For a number of years he would alternate between winters spent doing Western melodramas and summers out on the prairie.

His exploits on the Plains, especially his heroics during the Indian wars, made Bill even more notable. In 1883, Bill cashed in on his fame and started what would become the greatest Western show ever assembled: "Buffalo Bill's Wild West and Congress of Rough Riders of the World." This western-style circus was an instant success. Sometimes crowds of as many as 57,000 in one day came out to see the show. They weren't disappointed.

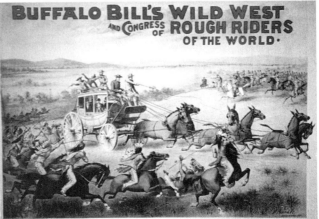

A publicity poster announcing Cody's Wild West show.

Stars of one of Buffalo Bill's many western dramas. From left to right: Elisha Green, James Butler "Wild Bill" Hickok, Buffalo Bill Cody, Texas Jack Omohundro, and Eugene Overton.

Cody chases a herd of buffalo around the field during a Wild West show.

The show was an amazing spectacle that included hundreds of authentic cowboys and Indians showing off their riding and roping skills and marksmanship. It had bucking broncos, Indian "raids," Pony Express demonstrations, an attack on the Deadwood stagecoach, and a mock buffalo hunt. Crowds went wild over little Annie Oakley, who could blast 100 small glass balls out of the sky and never miss. Another celebrity was Sioux Chief Sitting Bull.

At the center of this spectacle was Buffalo Bill himself, decked out in buckskin, riding a magnificent steed, a Stetson on his head and a six-shooter in his hand. The West was starting to fade by then, but Buffalo Bill was determined to keep the dream alive. For 30 years he toured with the company, taking his romantic vision of the Old West across this country and to Europe. In England he played before a royal gathering that included Queen Victoria.

A Beadle's Dime novel published in 1892.

Last of the Great Scouts

Touring with the Wild West show was difficult, a grueling job that lasted months at a time. But the money was good, allowing Cody to settle into the TE Ranch, which he built outside of Cody, Wyoming, and is still in existence today. During the off-season, Bill often spent time at the TE, hunting and tracking, getting back to the land he loved. In his later years, financial problems from the show weighed heavily on his mind; time spent at his ranch helped lift him out of his depression.

In 1913, Bill was forced to shut down the Wild West show after a run of 30 years. Much of the money he made was lost due to mismanagement. He had also invested poorly in a gold mine in Arizona, which never really panned out.

At age 67, Cody announced his retirement, with plans to settle down at his beloved TE Ranch in Wyoming. In true Cody style, however, he never could settle down in one place—touring with other Wild West shows around the country, or hosting friends and celebrities at the ranch in Wyoming, or taking them on distant hunting trips only Buffalo Bill could organize.

In a letter from Buffalo Bill to his cousin Lydia in 1894 he said, "I love children. Bring them all."

Buffalo Bill aboard his Arabian stallion, "Muson."

On January 10, 1917, Bill died at his sister May's home near Denver, Colorado after a brief illness. He was buried on top of nearby Lookout Mountain. His grave is now a popular tourist spot.

Every year, thousands come to pay tribute to the memory of this amazing man who symbolized the Old West for generations. William F. Cody. Buffalo Bill. Last of the great scouts.

Glossary

abolitionists

People who wanted an end to slavery in the United States.

break

A term used when taming wild horses, as in "to break a horse."

buffalo

A family of oxlike animals. In North America, the specific animal is technically called a bison, but is commonly referred to as a buffalo.

cavalry

Troops trained to fight on horseback. Today, cavalry troops have replaced horses with tanks and helicopters.

Civil War

In the United States, the war fought between armies of the North (the Union) and the South (the Confederacy) from 1861 to 1865. The war was fought for many reasons, the most important of which was the issue of slavery (see *abolitionists*). Also called the "War Between the States."

Custer, General George A. (1839–1876)

An American army officer and Indian fighter. He was a Union general in the Civil War. Custer died in 1876 at the Battle of the Little Bighorn.

Plains

Also called the Great Plains. Prairie lands extending from North Dakota to Texas, and from the Missouri River to the Rocky Mountains.

Pony Express

A system of mail transportation that used ponies in a series of relays. The Pony Express ran from St. Joseph, Missouri, to Sacramento, California from 1860 to 1861.

Queen Victoria (1819–1901)

Queen of the United Kingdom of Great Britain and Ireland from 1837 to 1901. Also the Empress of India from 1876 to 1901.

reservation

A section of land set aside by the United States government for use by an American Indian tribe or people.

scout

A person who goes ahead of the main part of a group, such as a military unit, to explore the land and gather information about the terrain or enemy ahead.

secesh

Slang term for "secessionist," a person who wanted the South (the Confederacy) to secede, or leave, the Union. (See Civil War.)

Sitting Bull, Chief (1834?–1890)

An American Indian chief of the Dakota Sioux tribe. Was a leader in the Sioux war from 1876 to 1877. Fought at the Battle of the Little Bighorn (see Custer), and in the ghost-dance uprising of 1890.

Springfield rifle

Chief weapon of the U.S. Army in its fight with the Plains Indians. Was faster loading and had more firepower than most other rifles of its time.

Bibliography

Brown, Dee. *Homage to Buffalo Bill.* National Geographic Traveler, Summer, 1984, pp. 46-51.

Cody, William F. *The Life of Buffalo Bill.* New York: Indian Head Books, 1991.

Encyclopaedia Britannica, Volume II, pp. 1,037-1,038.

Flanagan, Mike. *Out West.* New York: Harry N. Abrams, Inc., 1987.

Foote, Stella. *Letters from Buffalo Bill.* El Segundo, CA: Upton & Sons, 1990.

Hall, Alice. *Buffalo Bill and the Enduring West.* National Geographic, July, 1981, pp. 76-103.

Wheeler, Keith. *The Scouts.* New York: Time-Life Books, 1978.

Index